BRITISH
GHOSTS

TRUE GHOST STORIES FROM GREAT BRITAIN

DARK HOUSE PUBLISHING

CONTENTS

BRITISH GHOSTS

INTRODUCTION

Great Britain, with its long and storied history, is a land rich in tales of the paranormal. From the misty moors of Scotland to the ancient stones of England, and across the rolling hills of Wales, countless stories of eerie occurrences and haunting spirits have been whispered through the generations. The British Isles seem to be a breeding ground for tales that send a chill down the spine, whether you're a steadfast believer in the supernatural or a curious skeptic.

Journey into the heart of Britain's haunted past, where we will explore grand castles, humble cottages, prisons that have witnessed unspeakable suffering and scenic landscapes that hold dark secrets. We will recount tales of love that transcends the grave, of justice seeking to be served from beyond the veil, and of innocent souls caught in the restless realm between life and death.

Prepare to meet the Highgate Vampire, who lurks amongst the graves of the North London's Highgate Cemetery; the ghostly Drummer Boy of Edinburgh Castle, whose beats echo in the dead of night; and the spirits of executed prisoners that are said to haunt the Tower of London. These stories are woven into the fabric of Britain's history, creating a tapestry that is as haunting as it is fascinating.

As you read, consider the weight of history that these tales carry—the lives, the tragedies, the emotions that imbue each location with a spectral energy. Are these stories mere products of vivid imagination, fueled by the human fascination with the unknown? Or do they offer genuine glimpses into a world beyond our own, echoing with the voices of those long gone?

Whether you are reading by daylight or daring to delve into these tales by the flicker of candlelight, we invite you to journey with us. Let us step into Britain's haunted past together, traversing through time and space to explore the ghostly legends that are as much a part of British heritage as its historic landmarks.

In this collection, you will discover:

- **The Ghosts of Glastonbury Abbey**, where sacred hymns are said to echo through ruins steeped in spirituality and myth.
- **The Tragic Tale of the Grey Lady of Hampton Court**, forever wandering the halls of her former residence.
- **The Chilling Presence at the Ancient Ram Inn**, a place that some believe is the most haunted in all of England.
- **The Haunting of the Pendle Witches**, where the echoes of a 400-year-old witch trial reverberate to this day.

And many more tales that transport you to a Britain that exists in the tantalizing space between reality and the supernatural.

So, dear reader, as the nights draw in and the shadows lengthen, light a candle, pull your blanket tight, and join us as we explore the ghostly side of Britain – where history is alive, and quite possibly, looking back at you.

The Tower of London Ghosts

The Tower of London, one of the world's most iconic historical landmarks, is a place where history leaps off the pages of books and becomes an immersive experience.

But there is a lesser-known side to the Tower, a side that is whispered about in hushed tones: it is reputed to be one of the most haunted sites in all of Britain. From royal specters to tragic prisoners, the Tower of London seems to be a gathering place for the spirits of its dark and violent past.

A Royal Haunting: Anne Boleyn

Among the most famous of the Tower's alleged phantoms is Anne Boleyn, the second wife of King Henry VIII. After being accused of treason, she was executed on Tower Green in 1536. Reports say she has been seen wandering near the site of her death, sometimes with her head, sometimes without.

The Lost Princes

The chilling tale of the Princes in the Tower, Edward V and his younger brother Richard, is another dark chapter in the Tower's history. Allegedly murdered to prevent them from ascending the throne, they were reported missing and never found. Sightings of two young boys, described as appearing terrified, have been reported within the White Tower.

The White Lady

The White Tower, the oldest part of the complex, is said to be haunted by the White Lady. She has been seen waving to groups of schoolchildren, and her perfume is said to linger in the air.

Guards' Encounters

It's not just visitors who have reported ghostly sightings. Tower guards, known as Beefeaters, have reported numerous unexplained occurrences. One guard reported being attacked by an unseen force, which he initially thought to be a prank by his colleagues until he was nearly strangled by it.

The Weeping Lady

The ghost of Arbella Stuart, a cousin to Elizabeth I and James I, is said to haunt the Queen's House. She was imprisoned in the Tower by her cousin, King James I, and reports claim she can be heard weeping for her lost freedom and love.

Why So Haunted?

The Tower's bloody history makes it a prime candidate for haunting. Over its 1,000-year history, it has been a royal palace, a prison, and a place of execution. Many people met their end here under tragic and brutal circumstances, which some believe has left an indelible mark on the location.

A Paranormal Visit

For those interested in the paranormal, the Tower of London does not disappoint. Ghost tours are available, taking visitors through the sites of famous executions, past prisoners' quarters, and through the dimly lit stone hallways of the White Tower after dark. Guides regale visitors with tales of sightings and unexplained events.

The Skeptic's Perspective

Of course, it's worth noting that definitive proof of ghosts remains elusive. Skeptics might say that the eerie atmosphere of the ancient tower, combined with the tragic stories of those who died there, plays tricks on the minds of visitors and guards alike.

Whether you are a firm believer in the paranormal or a steadfast skeptic, there is no denying that the Tower of London holds a deep and lasting place in England's history. The stories of its ghosts are part of the rich tapestry that makes the Tower a fascinating place to visit. As you walk through the cold stone corridors, you are walking through history - and perhaps, just perhaps, you might feel the chill of a ghostly presence walking right along with you.

The Brown Lady of Raynham Hall

In the picturesque English countryside of Norfolk, there lies a grand, stately home with a long and intriguing history – Raynham Hall. This majestic mansion, which dates back to the 17th century, is famous not only for its grandeur but also for its most famous, and perhaps most unwelcome, resident: the Brown Lady.

The Legend Unveiled

The Brown Lady of Raynham Hall is one of the most famous ghost stories in Britain. She is believed to be the ghost of Lady Dorothy Walpole, the sister of Sir Robert Walpole, who is often regarded as the first Prime Minister of Great Britain. Lady Dorothy was married to Charles Townshend, who was notorious for his violent temper. Legend has it that when Townshend discovered his wife's infidelity, he locked her in the family estate, where she remained until her death in 1726 under mysterious circumstances.

The Iconic Photograph

In 1936, Raynham Hall gained worldwide attention when *Country Life* magazine published a photograph that appeared to show the ghostly figure of a woman descending the grand staircase. The figure in the photo was dubbed 'The Brown Lady' due to the brown brocade dress she appeared to be wearing. This photograph remains one of the most analyzed and debated ghost photos of all time.

Sightings Through the Years

There have been numerous reports of sightings of the Brown Lady. One of the most famous accounts is from King George IV, who, during his stay at Raynham Hall, claimed to have seen her standing beside his bed. Another famous sighting was by Colonel Loftus, who saw the Brown Lady one night while visiting the hall. He described her as wearing a brown satin dress, her face glowing with a light, her eyes empty sockets.

The Modern Day

Today, Raynham Hall is still a private residence, but the stories of the Brown Lady continue to attract ghost hunters, paranormal enthusiasts, and tourists alike. Despite the countless investigations and the famous photograph, no concrete evidence proving the existence of the Brown Lady has been presented, leaving room for skeptics to doubt.

The Skeptic's Corner

While the legend of the Brown Lady is captivating, skeptics have raised doubts about the authenticity of the famous photograph and other aspects of the story. Some believe the photograph to be the result of double exposure or an issue with the camera, while others argue that the entire legend is an imaginative tale woven through the years.

A Lasting Legacy

Whether you believe in ghosts or not, the tale of the Brown Lady of Raynham Hall remains a fascinating aspect of British folklore. Her story is a blend of tragic history, dark romance, and eerie mystery. It's a tale that continues to be told, a legend that adds a layer of mystique to the beautiful Raynham Hall.

Borley Rectory: England's Most Haunted House

Nestled in the quaint Essex countryside, the Borley Rectory was once dubbed the 'Most Haunted House in England'. This Victorian mansion, built in 1863, has since burned down and been demolished, but the stories surrounding it are as alive as ever.

What is it about the Borley Rectory that has fascinated paranormal enthusiasts for decades?

A Haunting Begins

The ghostly tales of Borley Rectory began almost as soon as it was built. The rectory was said to be haunted by a nun, who locals believe had fallen in love with a monk from the nearby monastery. Their love affair was discovered, and as punishment, the monk was executed, and the nun bricked up alive in the convent walls. Their spirits, along with others, were claimed to haunt the grounds of the rectory.

The Arrival of the Reverend

In 1928, Reverend Guy Eric Smith and his wife moved into the rectory. They reported a series of strange events, including the sounds of footsteps within the house, and a ghostly nun who was frequently seen at twilight. It was their reports that began to draw widespread attention to Borley Rectory.

Harry Price: The Ghost Hunter

In 1929, famed paranormal investigator Harry Price rented the rectory. His detailed logs of paranormal activity, including mysterious footsteps, cold spots, and a phantom carriage driven by two headless horsemen, brought Borley Rectory into the national spotlight. Price's books on the subject further solidified its reputation as the most haunted house in England.

A Fiery End

In 1939, the rectory caught fire and was severely damaged. During the blaze, witnesses reported seeing a figure in the window and various ghostly apparitions. After the fire, the remains of the house were demolished. Yet, strangely, reports of paranormal activity continued on the grounds where the rectory once stood.

Skepticism and Controversy

Harry Price's investigation has been a point of contention among skeptics. Critics argue that Price's claims were exaggerations, or even fabrications, designed to maintain public interest. After his death, some researchers suggested that Price planted fake phenomena.

The Legacy Today

While the Borley Rectory no longer stands, the site of the former building continues to be a place of interest for both ghost hunters and skeptics alike. People still report seeing the ghostly nun, hearing unexplained footsteps, and feeling a sudden drop in temperature.

The tale of Borley Rectory is one wrapped in mystery, intrigue, and controversy. Whether it was the imagination of those who lived there, a cleverly sustained hoax, or genuine paranormal activity, the story of Borley Rectory remains one of England's most captivating ghost stories. As you wander through the tranquil Essex countryside, perhaps you will sense the echoes of the past, still haunting the place where Borley Rectory once ominously stood.

The Pendle Witches

In the rolling hills of Lancashire, lies the sleepy village of Pendle. While the region is celebrated for its natural beauty, it's also known for a much darker piece of history. In 1612, it was the epicentre of England's most famous witch trial, where 12 people were accused of witchcraft. This is the haunting tale of the Pendle Witches.

A Time of Suspicion and Fear

In 17th century England, the fear of witches was real and widespread. King James I, a fervent believer in witchcraft, had passed an act that made it a capital offence. It was in this climate of paranoia that the story of the Pendle Witches unfolded.

The Accused

The Pendle Witches were a group of twelve individuals, including Elizabeth Southerns (also known as Demdike), her daughter Elizabeth Device, her grandchildren James and Alizon Device, and several others from the surrounding areas. They were ordinary people living in Pendle Hill, but they were about to become infamous.

The Alleged Crimes

In March 1612, Alizon Device was accused of cursing a peddler who subsequently suffered a stroke. This event was the spark that ignited the witch trials. Following this incident, other villagers came forward with accusations, claiming the alleged witches had been responsible for deaths, illness, and misfortune in the community for years.

The Trial

The trial of the Pendle Witches took place at Lancaster Castle. They were tried alongside the Samlesbury witches, accused by a 14-year-old girl, and others accused of witchcraft in York and Cheshire. The evidence presented against them was based mainly on the 'confessions' of the accused and the testimonies of neighbours. It's worth noting that these confessions were likely obtained under duress.

A Dark Verdict

Of the twelve accused, one was found not guilty. The remaining eleven were sentenced to death by hanging, and their executions were carried out on August 20, 1612. The trial is one of the most notorious witchcraft trials in English history.

A Lasting Legacy

Today, the tale of the Pendle Witches is a significant chapter in the history of witchcraft persecution. It is a vivid example of how fear and paranoia can lead to tragic consequences. The story of the Pendle Witches is remembered as a cautionary tale, a dark period when justice was overshadowed by superstition and fear.

Pendle Today

Now, Pendle has embraced its witchy history and has become a destination for those interested in the darker side of England's past. Each year, tourists are drawn to the scenic Lancashire countryside to visit the sites associated with the Pendle Witches, including Lancaster Castle, where the trial took place, and Pendle Hill itself.

The story of the Pendle Witches is a poignant reminder of a turbulent time in England's history, where superstition and fear led to the death of innocent people. While the beautiful landscape of Pendle now seems a world away from the dark events of 1612, the tale of the Pendle Witches continues to captivate and haunt those who delve into this grim chapter of England's past.

The Ghosts of Pluckley Village

The charming village of Pluckley, Kent, is known for its scenic vistas and quaint historic buildings, but also holds a more eerie distinction — it is reputedly the most haunted village in England.

From phantom monks to screaming men, let's uncover the ghostly tales that shroud Pluckley in mystery.

A Village with a Haunting Reputation

Pluckley's reputation as a haunted hotspot isn't just local folklore; in 1989, the Guinness Book of Records awarded it the title of 'the most haunted village in England'. With up to 16 reported ghosts, Pluckley is steeped in supernatural tales that attract ghost hunters, paranormal enthusiasts, and curious visitors alike.

The Red Lady of Pluckley

One of the most famous phantoms is the Red Lady, said to be the ghost of Lady Dering. According to local legends, she was buried in a red rose-covered coffin in the 12th century. Visitors to St Nicholas Church have reported sightings of a woman in a red dress, often seen wandering the churchyard with a mournful expression.

The Screaming Man

Another of Pluckley's infamous apparitions is the Screaming Man, believed to be the ghost of a brickworker who fell to his death at the Pinnock Bridge. Passers-by have reported hearing terrifying, agonizing screams near this spot, particularly on misty mornings.

The Phantom Monk of Greystones

Greystones, a residential house dating back to the 18th century, is said to be haunted by the ghost of a monk. The spirit is often seen in the early hours of the morning, wearing a long, dark robe, and seems to be searching for something or someone.

The Wandering Highwayman

The ghost of a highwayman who met a grisly end at Fright Corner is another staple of Pluckley's paranormal lore. He was reportedly pinned to a tree and killed with a sword. Today, visitors claim to have seen a shadowy figure lurking at the scene, still seemingly stuck in his final, fatal moment.

A Skeptic's Perspective

While the tales of Pluckley's ghosts are famous far and wide, skeptics point out the lack of concrete evidence. Some argue that the stories have been embellished over time, evolving into more fantastical versions that are far removed from any original events. But for those who have experienced something inexplicable in Pluckley, skepticism is a hard pill to swallow.

Pluckley Today: A Haunting Tourist Attraction

Today, Pluckley embraces its haunted reputation, attracting a steady stream of tourists eager to experience England's most haunted village for themselves.

Guided ghost tours are a popular activity, offering visitors a detailed account of the village's spooky history and a chance to potentially encounter a ghostly resident.

This small hamlet in the heart of Kent, with its rolling fields and historic charm, is a place where the past feels unusually close, as though the villagers of yesteryear never quite left.

For a truly unique and potentially spine-tingling experience, a visit to Pluckley is a must.

The Edinburgh Vaults: Scotland's Spookiest Subterranean City

Beneath the bustling streets of Scotland's historic capital lies a shadowy, subterranean world. Known as the Edinburgh Vaults, this labyrinth of chambers and passageways has a dark and storied past.

Today, it is considered one of the most haunted locations in the UK.

A Glimpse into the Past

Built in the late 18th century beneath the South Bridge, the Edinburgh Vaults were initially intended as storage spaces for businesses. However, as time passed, they became home to some of the city's poorest residents and a hotbed of criminal activity. Living conditions were dire, with no access to sunlight or fresh air, and the vaults became a breeding ground for disease.

The Ghost of the Watchful Cobbler

One of the most frequently reported spirits in the vaults is that of a cobbler. Visitors have reported feeling a presence closely watching them, accompanied by the distinct smell of leather. Some claim to have seen an apparition of a man in period clothing, complete with tools of the cobbler's trade.

The Wailing Child of the Vaults

In the dank and dark vaults, the cries of a child are especially unnerving. Many visitors have reported hearing the heart-wrenching sobs of a young girl, named by some as 'Annie'. It is believed she died here from the plague, and her sorrowful spirit remains. In response to her sad tale, visitors often leave dolls and toys to comfort her spirit.

The Aggressive Entity

Not all the entities reported in the vaults are benign. There have been accounts of an aggressive male spirit, particularly in a section known as 'Mr. Boots' room'. People have reported being pushed, touched, or feeling a sudden chill. The ghost, nicknamed 'Mr. Boots', is said to be the spirit of a violent and sinister man who lived in the vaults during the 18th century.

Paranormal Investigations and Experiences

The Edinburgh Vaults have drawn numerous paranormal investigators, eager to document the alleged activity within this underground city. From EVP (Electronic Voice Phenomena) recordings capturing unexplained voices to ghostly figures caught on camera, the evidence, though controversial, is tantalizing for believers.

Exploring the Edinburgh Vaults Today

Today, visitors to Edinburgh can explore the vaults on guided tours, which range from historical walks to dedicated ghost tours. Walking through the vaults, with their damp, cold air and eerie echoes, it's easy to feel transported back to a darker time – and to believe that something supernatural lingers.

A Skeptic's Perspective

While the chilling tales of the Edinburgh Vaults captivate many, skeptics question the authenticity of these stories. They point to the power of suggestion, the ambiance of the location, and the natural desire to experience something paranormal as explanations for the reports of ghostly encounters.

Chillingham Castle

Standing tall amidst the Northumbrian countryside, Chillingham Castle has been a silent witness to England's history for over 800 years.

With its medieval architecture, secret passageways, and tales of torture and tragedy, it's no surprise that Chillingham Castle is reputed to be one of the most haunted places in

A Castle Steeped in History

Originally a monastery in the 12th century, Chillingham Castle has a storied history, including its role as a stronghold during the Anglo-Scottish Wars. Its dark past includes gruesome tales of battle, betrayal, and a notorious torture chamber that has been preserved to this day.

The Blue Boy: A Tragic Apparition

One of the most renowned spirits of Chillingham Castle is the Blue Boy. According to legend, visitors have reported seeing a blue halo of light near a portrait in the Pink Room. It is believed to be the ghost of a boy who was found dead in a wall during renovation work, surrounded by blue clothing and papers that proved his noble birth.

The White Pantry Ghost

In the castle's Inner Pantry, a frail figure in white has often been reported. She is believed to be a forlorn woman who, in life, was the pantry keeper. Visitors have reported feeling her presence, cold spots, and even a hand grabbing at them, seemingly in search of something stolen from her pantry.

The Torturer of the Dungeon

The castle's terrifying torture chamber, which remains almost exactly as it was over 500 years ago, is said to be haunted by John Sage, a notorious torturer from the days of King Edward I. Visitors to the chamber have reported feeling sudden, unexplained pain, hearing anguished cries, and sensing an ominous presence.

The Weeping Lady of the Chapel

In the castle's chapel, there are frequent reports of a spectral woman weeping bitterly. She is believed to be the ghost of Lady Mary Berkeley, whose husband left her for her sister. It is said that her sorrowful spirit still mourns her lost love.

Paranormal Investigations at Chillingham

In recent years, Chillingham Castle has become a hotspot for paranormal investigators. From EVP sessions capturing ghostly voices to unexplained cold spots and eerie photographs, these investigations have added a new chapter to the castle's haunting legacy.

Visiting the Castle Today

For those brave enough, Chillingham Castle is open for visitors and even offers overnight stays. Ghost tours led by experienced guides narrate the castle's history and its ghostly tales, giving visitors a chance to walk the rooms and hallways that have been the setting for so many stories of the supernatural.

Skeptic or Believer?

While the tales of Chillingham Castle's ghosts are famous and chilling, skeptics point to the power of suggestion and the castle's dark history as explanations for the paranormal claims.

Yet, for those who have experienced inexplicable phenomena within the castle's walls, the ghosts of Chillingham are all too real.

As you wander through its stone hallways, you might just find that the line between legend and reality becomes eerily blurred.

The Ancient Ram Inn

In the charming village of Wotton-under-Edge, Gloucestershire, stands a seemingly modest, timeworn building. Known as the Ancient Ram Inn, this structure is anything but ordinary.

With a history stretching back over 1,000 years, it is reputed to be one of the most haunted locations in England.

A History Entwined with Mystery

The Ancient Ram Inn, built in 1145, was originally intended to be a priest's dwelling. It has served various purposes throughout the years, from an inn to a private residence. Many believe that its location, purportedly built on an ancient pagan burial ground, is the source of the intense paranormal activity reported here.

The Witch's Room and Her Tragic Fate

One of the Inn's most notorious rooms is the 'Witch's Room'. Legend has it that a woman sought refuge in this room in the 1500s but was later captured and burned as a witch. Today, visitors claim to feel a heavy energy in this room, and some report seeing the apparition of a distressed woman.

The Terrifying Tale of the Bishop's Room

Often described as the most haunted room in the Inn, the Bishop's Room is said to be home to several spirits. Guests who have dared to spend a night here have reported being touched or pulled by unseen hands, sudden drops in temperature, and hearing unexplained footsteps and knocking sounds.

The Ghost of a Murdered Child

In one haunting account, the skeletal remains of children were reportedly found under the staircase during renovation work, along with a broken dagger. Could this be the source of the ghostly cries that guests report hearing through the dark, still nights at the Inn?

The Current Keeper of the Ghostly Inn

Until his passing, John Humphries, the last private owner of the Ancient Ram Inn, was a significant figure in its story. He claimed to have experienced intense and frightening paranormal activity from the first night he spent in the property. His tales of confrontation with the supernatural are integral to the modern mythology of the Inn.

Paranormal Investigations at the Ancient Ram Inn

Due to its eerie reputation, the Ancient Ram Inn has attracted ghost hunters and paranormal enthusiasts for years. From EVP (Electronic Voice Phenomena) recordings capturing disembodied voices to mysterious orbs and shadow figures caught on camera, the Inn continues to be a focal point for investigations into the unknown.

Visiting the Haunted Dwelling

If you have a taste for the supernatural and a strong constitution, you can visit the Ancient Ram Inn. Though no longer operating as a B&B, the Inn is often open for pre-booked guided tours, where you'll be regaled with its history, legends, and firsthand accounts of paranormal experiences.

Skeptic's Perspective

While tales of haunting at the Ancient Ram Inn are widespread, skeptics question the authenticity of these stories. They suggest that the Inn's ancient and creeky architecture, combined with its dark history, sets the stage for imagined ghostly encounters.

This old building, with its sagging timbers and windswept location, evokes an eerie atmosphere that appeals to anyone drawn to the mysteries of the past.

The Grey Lady of Hampton Court

Hampton Court Palace in Surrey is renowned as one of the most majestic royal residences in Britain. But beyond its grand halls and exquisite gardens lies a more mysterious and ghostly tale.

Among the various spectres said to haunt Hampton Court, none is as well-known as the Grey Lady.

A Palace Rich with History

Built in the 16th century, Hampton Court Palace is a grand building with a storied past. Originally built for Cardinal Thomas Wolsey, it later became one of King Henry VIII's favourite residences. Today, it stands as a testament to Tudor grandeur and subsequent royal eras—but it also houses its share of spectral stories.

The Grey Lady: A Brief Introduction

The Grey Lady, believed by some to be the ghost of Sybil Penn, is one of Hampton Court's most famous phantoms. Sybil Penn was a servant and nurse to Prince Edward, son of Henry VIII and his third wife Jane Seymour. When Prince Edward fell ill in 1552, Sybil cared for him until her own death due to smallpox, which she contracted while nursing the prince.

The Unearthed Tomb and a Resurgent Spirit

Sybil Penn was initially buried in the nearby church of St. Mary's, but her tomb was disturbed during 19th-century renovations. According to the tales, this disruption caused her spirit to become restless, and reports of sightings at Hampton Court began shortly thereafter.

Sightings and Sounds: The Presence of the Grey Lady

Visitors and staff have reported seeing a lady in a grey dress throughout the corridors of Hampton Court. More intriguing are the accounts of eerie sounds, notably a distinct, repetitive noise resembling the act of spinning.

In a striking coincidence, a forgotten chamber of the palace discovered later was found to contain an antique spinning wheel.

Hampton Court: A Paranormal Hotspot

The Grey Lady is not the only ghost said to haunt Hampton Court. From Catherine Howard, Henry VIII's fifth wife, to Jane Seymour, his third wife, the palace is alleged to host several royal spectres— each with a tale as tragic and intriguing as the last.

A Walk through Haunted Halls

For those looking to experience the chill of a ghostly presence, Hampton Court Palace is open to the public and offers various tours. The palace does a wonderful job of blending history with the mystery, making for a captivating visit.

The Skeptic's Perspective

While the stories of the Grey Lady and other Hampton Court phantoms are enthralling, skeptics point to the power of suggestion and the rich, dramatic history of the palace as the source of these tales. Without concrete evidence, the stories remain fascinating legends.

Whether you're a history buff, a fan of royal drama, or a seeker of the supernatural, Hampton Court Palace offers a rich and multifaceted experience.

As you wander through its opulent rooms and along its grand corridors, keep an eye out for the Grey Lady.

Whether legend or reality, her tale is woven into the very fabric of this remarkable royal residence, adding a layer of intrigue that makes a visit to Hampton Court truly unforgettable.

The Hound of Dartmoor

The vast and windswept moors of Dartmoor in Devon, are a place of natural beauty, historic fascination, and rich folklore.

Among the tales that have emerged from its misty expanses is that of a creature as chilling as it is captivating: The Hound of Dartmoor.

A Moor Shrouded in Mystery

Dartmoor, with its rugged terrain, ancient stone circles, and misty atmosphere, has long been a source of inspiration for legends and stories. It's a place where imagination can run wild, much like the creature said to roam its hills.

The Legend of the Hound

For centuries, locals and visitors alike have reported sightings of a large and fearsome black dog haunting the moors. Descriptions paint the Hound of Dartmoor as an unusually large and powerful creature, with glowing red eyes and a terrifying howl that can freeze the blood of anyone unlucky enough to hear it.

A Literary Immortalisation

The Hound of Dartmoor is widely believed to have inspired Sir Arthur Conan Doyle's classic novel, *The Hound of the Baskervilles*. In his tale, Sherlock Holmes investigates a supernatural hound that has been the curse of the Baskerville family for generations. Doyle's narrative brings a vivid, eerie life to this legendary creature.

Sightings and Encounters

Reports of encounters with the Hound are numerous. Some witnesses describe a creature resembling a massive dog, while others suggest a more supernatural entity. Notably, the Hound is often associated with specific locations, such as Hound Tor and the Grimspound Bronze Age settlement.

Natural Explanations

Skeptics of the Dartmoor legend propose several more mundane explanations for the Hound. Some suggest that witnesses are mistaking large, native dogs for the creature, while others believe that the region's wild and remote environment can play tricks on the eyes and mind, especially in low light.

The Hound in Modern Culture

The Hound of Dartmoor has transcended local folklore to become a part of broader British culture. It has inspired books, movies, and documentaries, each reimagining the legend in a new light. Whether as a spectral beast or a symbol of the wild, untamed nature of Dartmoor itself, the Hound continues to capture imaginations.

A Journey to the Heart of Dartmoor

For those brave enough to walk the moors themselves, Dartmoor National Park is open to the public and offers a variety of walking trails and guided tours. Whether or not you encounter the Hound, a visit to Dartmoor is a profound experience, rich with natural beauty and historical depth.

A Legend that Endures

Whether myth, misidentification, or something more supernatural, the Hound of Dartmoor is a legend that endures. It's a story that captures the imagination, much like Dartmoor itself—a vast, wild place that feels, in many ways, like a land out of time.

The Hound of Dartmoor is a legend that weaves together the natural drama of Dartmoor's landscape with the darker corners of our imagination. Whether you're a seeker of the supernatural or simply someone who appreciates the deep and fascinating tapestry of British folklore, the tale of the Hound is an intriguing chapter in the story of this ancient, awe-inspiring place.

The Ghost of Samlesbury Hall

Samlesbury Hall stands as a stunning example of a medieval manor house. Yet, within its historic walls, whispers of a haunting tale persist — the ghost of Samlesbury Hall.

A Manor House Steeped in History

Samlesbury Hall, built in the 14th century, is one of the most enduring historic homes in England. With its sumptuous interiors and stunning woodwork, it offers a fascinating glimpse into the past.

But for some visitors, the past appears to be more living than they might have imagined.

Lady Dorothy Southworth: A Tragic Tale

Central to the ghostly tales of Samlesbury Hall is the figure of Lady Dorothy Southworth, also known as 'Dolly'. According to legend, Lady Dorothy fell in love with a man of a rival family in the 17th century.

When her love affair was discovered by her family, her lover was murdered, and Lady Dorothy was reportedly driven to madness by the tragic event.

It is believed that her restless spirit now wanders the grounds and halls of Samlesbury.

Sightings of a Forlorn Spirit

Visitors and staff at Samlesbury Hall have reported seeing the ghostly figure of a woman, believed to be Lady Dorothy, roaming the premises.

Sightings are often accompanied by a profound sense of sadness, and she is usually seen in the late evening, wandering the corridors and the beautiful Queen Anne Chapel.

Whispers in the Hall

Beyond sightings of Lady Dorothy's apparition, some visitors have reported hearing soft, sorrowful whispering and crying when the hall is quiet, further fuelling the lore surrounding her tragic tale.

The Historical Facts

While the ghost story is a compelling tale, historical records regarding Lady Dorothy Southworth and the details of her tragic love story are sketchy, leading some to believe that her story may be a piece of local folklore rather than a factual account.

Paranormal Investigations at Samlesbury Hall

The stories of Lady Dorothy's ghost have drawn paranormal investigators from around the world.

While some claim to have recorded evidence of her presence, others leave with nothing but the chilling atmosphere of the ancient hall.

Visiting the Hauntingly Beautiful Samlesbury Hall

Samlesbury Hall, now a charitable trust, is open to the public. Visitors can explore the historic rooms, walk through the lush gardens, and perhaps, if they are so inclined, keep an eye out for Lady Dorothy. The hall also offers guided tours, including a 'Ghost Tour' for those curious about its paranormal past.

A Skeptic's Viewpoint

While the ghostly tales of Samlesbury Hall captivate many, skeptics suggest that the tales are born from the hall's long and dramatic history, rather than any actual hauntings.

The eerie atmosphere of a 14th-century hall can easily play tricks on the mind, they argue.

Samlesbury Hall offers a unique and enchanting visit. The tale of Lady Dorothy, with its blend of love, tragedy, and haunting, adds an undeniable mystique to this magnificent Lancashire landmark.

The Screaming Skull of Burton Agnes Hall

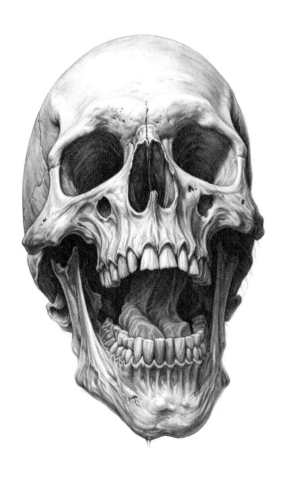

Burton Agnes Hall is a beautiful Elizabethan manor house in the scenic countryside of East Yorkshire. But behind its grand façade lies a chilling tale, one that has lingered in the local folklore for centuries – the legend of the Screaming Skull of Burton Agnes Hall.

A Majestic Manor with a Mysterious Tale

Constructed between 1598 and 1610 by Sir Henry Griffith, Burton Agnes Hall is an architectural marvel, listed as a Grade I building in the English Heritage register.

Yet, its architectural beauty is equally matched by the eerie tale of a certain skull that, according to legend, protects the peace of the house.

The Tragic Story of Anne Griffith

The tale begins with Anne Griffith, one of the daughters of Sir Henry Griffith.

As the story goes, Anne was violently attacked during a visit to a nearby location. She managed to return to Burton Agnes Hall but succumbed to her injuries soon after.

On her deathbed, she reportedly expressed a wish for her head to remain within the home she loved so dearly.

The Unsettled Skull

Ignoring Anne's dying wish, her family laid her to rest in a nearby church. Soon after, unsettling phenomena began.

Strange noises, believed to be Anne's screams, filled the hall, and unexplained disturbances plagued the household.

Desperate for peace, the family is said to have exhumed Anne's body, finding her skull detached from her skeleton. They brought the skull back to the hall, and the disturbances ceased.

The Enshrined Relic

Since the return of the skull, peace reportedly reigned over Burton Agnes Hall. To this day, it is said that the skull is hidden within the walls of the manor.

Numerous owners have supposedly attempted to remove it, each time resulting in eerie disturbances until the skull was replaced.

Visiting Burton Agnes Hall

Today, Burton Agnes Hall is a major tourist attraction, boasting stunning gardens and an impressive art collection.

The house warmly welcomes visitors to explore its grand rooms and beautiful grounds — and perhaps to feel the lingering presence of Anne Griffith.

A Skeptic's Perspective

While the story of the Screaming Skull is a chilling and memorable tale, skeptics argue that it is just that — a tale.

There are no contemporary records of Anne Griffith's tragic attack, and the skull itself has never been publicly displayed, leading some to question the truth of the story.

The Legacy of the Screaming Skull

Regardless of its veracity, the tale of the Screaming Skull of Burton Agnes Hall has become a significant part of the estate's history.

It's a story that visitors still ask about and one that adds a layer of mystique to this already enchanting property.

The Screaming Skull of Burton Agnes Hall is a tale that combines history, family tragedy, and the supernatural in one compelling narrative.

Whether you are a seeker of the paranormal or a lover of historical architecture, a visit to Burton Agnes Hall promises not only a glimpse into the grandeur of the Elizabethan era but also a touch of the mysterious that will linger long after you leave.

BRITISH GHOSTS

The Ghost of Mary Queen of Scots

Just outside Edinburgh, stands the majestic Borthwick Castle. This 15th-century fortress, steeped in history and architectural beauty, is said to host a very royal ghost—Mary, Queen of Scots.

A Castle with Regal Ties

Borthwick Castle, built in 1430, is one of the best-preserved medieval castles in Scotland. Its rich history is deeply tied to numerous significant figures, but none as captivating as Mary, Queen of Scots, who sought refuge here in the 16th century during a tumultuous period of her life.

Mary's Dramatic Escape

In 1567, Mary, Queen of Scots, and her third husband, James Hepburn, Earl of Bothwell, took refuge in Borthwick Castle while fleeing from forces loyal to the Scottish nobility.

During her stay, the castle came under siege, forcing Mary to make a daring escape, allegedly dressed as a page, to evade capture.

A Queen's Apparition

For centuries, reports have circulated that Mary's spirit lingers at Borthwick Castle. Guests and staff have claimed to have seen a ghostly figure, wearing a flowing gown, moving through the castle's rooms and hallways.

This apparition is believed to be Mary, her presence forever tied to the place of her dramatic escape.

Whispers and Phantom Footsteps

In addition to sightings of the spectral queen, visitors have reported hearing unexplained sounds—soft whispers, the rustle of a gown, and footsteps echoing through the stone halls when no one else is present.

These phenomena are said to be most common in Mary's Room, where the queen herself once slept.

Borthwick Castle Today

Now a luxurious hotel, Borthwick Castle welcomes guests from around the world, inviting them to sleep within its historic walls, dine like lords and ladies of old, and perhaps encounter its royal ghost.

Mary's Room, a lavish suite, is a particularly popular choice for visitors keen to experience the castle's paranormal side.

A Skeptic's Perspective

While the ghost story is a beloved part of Borthwick Castle's lore, skeptics point out the lack of concrete evidence supporting these supernatural claims.

They argue that the tales are likely a blend of history and myth, amplified by the castle's naturally eerie atmosphere.

The Enduring Legend

Regardless of one's stance on the paranormal, the story of Mary, Queen of Scots, and her connection to Borthwick Castle is undeniably fascinating.

The tale has become a significant aspect of the castle's identity, adding a layer of mystery and romance that captivates visitors to this day.

Glastonbury Abbey

The ruins of Glastonbury Abbey can be found deep in the heart of the Somerset countryside. This once grand and magnificent monastery, steeped in legend and spirituality, is said to be home to several ethereal inhabitants.

Join us as we explore the captivating tales of the ghosts of Glastonbury Abbey.

A Sacred and Ancient Site

Glastonbury Abbey was one of the most important Christian monastic communities in England before the Dissolution of the Monasteries in the 16th century.

Beyond its Christian history, Glastonbury is also a place of legend, purportedly the resting place of King Arthur and a candidate for the mystical Isle of Avalon.

The Phantom Monk of Glastonbury

One of the most frequently reported ghost sightings at the Abbey is that of an ethereal monk.

Dressed in traditional monk's robes, this spirit is said to wander the ruins, especially around the Abbot's Kitchen, which stands relatively intact compared to the rest of the abbey.

The Lady of the Abbey

Another renowned spectral figure is a mysterious woman, known as the Lady of the Abbey. Visitors have reported seeing her gracefully walking through the ruins, often described as being dressed in long, flowing garments, giving off a peaceful aura.

The Ghost of King Arthur

While the legendary King Arthur's historical existence is a subject of debate, the legend of Arthur and Glastonbury Abbey are intricately linked.

The ghostly figure of a tall and kingly man, presumed to be Arthur, has been reported standing solemnly near the site where the legendary King and his Queen, Guinevere, are said to be buried.

Haunting Melodies

Beyond the apparitions, some visitors have reported hearing the ethereal sounds of sacred hymns and chanting. These haunting melodies, reminiscent of a choir, are said to fill the air during the early hours of dawn or at dusk, adding to the mystical atmosphere of the site.

Modern Pilgrims and Paranormal Enthusiasts

Today, Glastonbury Abbey attracts a diverse group of visitors, from spiritual seekers and history enthusiasts to those intrigued by the paranormal. For those interested in the eerie, guided ghost tours provide an opportunity to explore the abbey's history and its otherworldly tales after dark.

A Skeptic's Perspective

While the ghost stories associated with Glastonbury Abbey are intriguing and add to the site's mystical ambiance, skeptics argue that the stories are born from the abbey's rich history and the human propensity for seeing patterns, especially in a place imbued with such spiritual significance.

The Legacy of Glastonbury Abbey

Whether or not one believes in the supernatural, the ruins of Glastonbury Abbey are undeniably atmospheric. The blend of deep history, legend, and ghostly tales makes it a fascinating place, where the past feels eerily close to the present.

The Glastonbury Abbey ghosts are more than just tales; they are part of a rich a mystical history that makes this place extraordinary.

Whether you walk the abbey grounds in search of spiritual connection, historical insight, or a brush with the supernatural, Glastonbury Abbey remains one of England's most captivating and enigmatic sites.

The Canewdon Witches

In the quaint rural village of Canewdon in Essex, a rich and dark history is whispered with the winds that sweep across its fields. According to legend, this seemingly peaceful village is inextricably linked with witchcraft, a connection that dates back several centuries.

We delve into the eerie tales of the Canewdon Witches and explore how this small village became synonymous with sorcery.

The Prophecy of the Canewdon Witches

The story of the Canewdon Witches is heavily tied to a prophecy made by the infamous 16th-century witchfinder, Matthew Hopkins. It is said that he proclaimed, "There will always be six witches in Canewdon." According to local folklore, as long as the steeple of St Nicholas Church stands, so will the presence of witches in Canewdon.

The Witch Trials

In the 16th and 17th centuries, England was swept by a wave of witch trials, and Canewdon was no exception. The most notable case was perhaps that of George Pickingill, a cunning man who was said to have been a powerful warlock with nine witch disciples. His legacy is a source of both local pride and eerie fascination.

The Haunting Presence

Visitors and residents alike have reported various paranormal occurrences, from seeing the ghost of a 'cunning woman' near the church to hearing mysterious footsteps and feeling sudden, unexplained chills.

These tales have only served to solidify Canewdon's reputation as a village where the spectral and the real coexist.

The Modern-Day Legacy

Today, Canewdon is a peaceful and charming village, but its witchy history is a significant aspect of local culture. Every year, around Halloween, it becomes a focal point for both curious visitors and modern-day witches who feel a spiritual connection to the place.

Skeptic or Believer?

As with all legends, the stories of the Canewdon witches are a blend of fact and fiction. There are real, documented cases of individuals who were accused of witchcraft, but the more supernatural elements of the legends are harder to substantiate. Skeptics argue that the tales are merely stories, born from a time of superstition and fear.

The tales of the Canewdon Witches are a poignant reminder of a darker time in England's history, where fear and superstition led to the persecution of the innocent. Today, these stories form a vital part of Canewdon's rich cultural tapestry, drawing visitors from far and wide to this small village with a big history.

Whether visiting the historic St Nicholas Church, walking the serene pathways that crisscross the village, or participating in one of Canewdon's famed ghost walks, this village is a living testament to England's complex relationship with its witching past.

So, the next time you find yourself in Essex, consider a trip to Canewdon—a place where history, legend, and perhaps a touch of the supernatural, converge in the most enchanting way.

The Highgate Vampire

Highgate Cemetery, an iconic Victorian burial ground in North London, is known not only for its stunning Gothic architecture but also as the setting of one of the most intriguing urban legends of the 20th century: the Highgate Vampire.

The Birth of a Legend

In the early 1970s, reports began to surface about strange occurrences in Highgate Cemetery. People claimed to have seen a dark figure with piercing red eyes lurking among the graves.

Animals were found drained of blood. This sequence of eerie reports gave rise to the legend of the Highgate Vampire, a supposed king of the undead who had awakened from his slumber.

A Media Sensation

The story soon caught the attention of the British press. Newspapers were filled with eye-witness accounts and speculation.

Fuelled by the media, a frenzy developed around the cemetery, drawing curious onlookers, vampire hunters, and paranormal investigators.

The Duel of the Vampire Hunters

At the center of the spectacle were two men, Sean Manchester and David Farrant, who both claimed to be professional vampire hunters.

Their public rivalry, each claiming that they alone could vanquish the Highgate Vampire, only intensified the public's fascination with the story. Their duel became a legendary part of the Highgate narrative.

The Reality Behind the Myth

Skeptics argue that the Highgate Vampire was nothing more than a product of the era's fascination with the occult, coupled with the dramatic, decaying elegance of Highgate Cemetery itself.

Some believe that the sightings were a result of mass hysteria, fuelled by the media and the dramatic claims of Manchester and Farrant.

Highgate Today

Highgate Cemetery has since become a popular tourist attraction, known for its beautiful and haunting atmosphere. Visitors from all over the world come to see the final resting places of famous figures such as Karl Marx and George Eliot, and perhaps, to catch a glimpse of the legendary vampire.

The Highgate Vampire legend is a captivating blend of history, hysteria, and modern myth-making. Whether it was the work of an overactive collective imagination or something more sinister, the tale of the Highgate Vampire endures as one of London's most chilling and enduring urban legends.

As you wander the serene, ivy-clad pathways of Highgate Cemetery, it is hard to imagine the frenzy that once gripped this place.

But as dusk falls and shadows lengthen, one can almost understand how, in the right light, the cemetery could become the setting for one of London's most famous supernatural tales.

The Phantom Roman Legion of York

In the ancient city of York, England—a place steeped in history and layered with stories—one legend stands out starkly from the rest.

It is a tale of spectral soldiers from a distant past, forever bound to march through the underbelly of the city: the Phantom Roman Legion of York.

The Ghostly Sightings

The legend of the Phantom Roman Legion centers around an extraordinary incident that took place in 1953. A local plumber, Harry Martindale, was installing a new heating system in the cellars of the Treasurer's House when he heard a distant horn. Suddenly, a Roman soldier materialized, followed by more - an entire legion, marching past him, seemingly unaware of his presence. Martindale later identified them as the Roman Ninth Legion by the markings on their shields.

A City Steeped in Roman History

York, or 'Eboracum' as it was known during Roman times, was once a significant Roman stronghold in Britain. It was the seat of power from which emperors ruled and where some even met their end.

The Ninth Legion, known as 'Legio IX Hispana,' was a real Roman Legion that mysteriously disappeared from records in the 2nd century AD. Theories about their fate abound, but no conclusive evidence has been found.

Eerily Accurate Details

What makes Martindale's account compelling is the precise detail with which he described the soldiers and their attire. He noted that they appeared cut off at the knee, but as he observed, the floor he was working on had been significantly raised since Roman times—they were marching on their original ground level.

More Than Just a Story?

Martindale's experience is not an isolated one. Over the years, numerous other sightings of the ghostly Roman soldiers have been reported in York, mostly in the vicinity of the Treasurer's House. These reports have added a layer of credibility to an already chilling tale, making it one of the most famous ghost stories in the UK.

The Treasurer's House Today

Today, the Treasurer's House is a well-preserved historic site and a popular tourist attraction managed by the National Trust. Visitors can explore the house and its cellars, where guides are more than happy to recount the tale of the Phantom Roman Legion and other ghost stories associated with the property.

The Phantom Roman Legion of York is a tale that interweaves history, myth, and a dash of eerie reality. Is it a vivid glimpse into the city's ancient past, a trick of the light, or pure legend? We may never know for sure.

What we do know is that York is a city with a past that is still very much alive, whether in the form of beautifully preserved architecture, rich historical records, or the spectral soldiers that, legend has it, still march beneath its streets.

So, as you walk through the historic sites of York, you may want to listen closely. You might just hear the distant sound of a Roman horn and the march of soldiers from a time long past.

The Ghosts of Blickling Hall

Blickling Hall, a majestic Jacobean mansion in Norfolk with a history as rich and deep as its sprawling estate.

While its grand architecture and beautiful gardens attract thousands of visitors each year, Blickling Hall holds another, more eerie, distinction. It is said to be one of the most haunted houses in England.

The Most Famous Phantom: Anne Boleyn

The most notorious ghost said to haunt Blickling Hall is Anne Boleyn, the ill-fated second wife of King Henry VIII. Although historians debate whether she was actually born at Blickling, the estate is strongly associated with the Boleyn family. Legend has it that every year, on the anniversary of her execution (May 19), Anne's ghost arrives at the Hall in a carriage drawn by a headless horseman. She, too, is said to be headless, holding her severed head securely in her lap.

Sir John Fastolf: The Knight in Shining Armour

Another prominent ghost believed to roam the grounds is Sir John Fastolf, a 15th-century knight who served during the Hundred Years' War. Although Fastolf had no direct links to Blickling Hall, he hailed from Norfolk and some believe that his spirit returned to his native county in death.

The Grey Lady of Blickling

Adding to the estate's haunted reputation is the so-called 'Grey Lady,' believed to be the spirit of Lady Mary Hobart, a former resident of the house. Staff and visitors alike have reported seeing her gliding through the library, where her portrait also hangs.

Paranormal Investigations

Given its reputation, it is no surprise that Blickling Hall has attracted paranormal investigators from around the world. Numerous teams have explored the hall and its grounds, armed with equipment designed to detect supernatural activity. While some visitors leave convinced of the hall's haunted nature, others regard these ghostly tales as nothing more than engaging stories.

Blickling Hall Today

Now managed by the National Trust, Blickling Hall is a treasured historic site, celebrated for its stunning architecture, priceless art collections, and meticulously maintained gardens.

However, the ghost stories remain a significant part of Blickling's allure, and the estate embraces its haunted reputation, especially around Halloween, when it hosts various spooky events.

BRITISH GHOSTS

The Drummer Boy of Edinburgh Castle

Perched atop Castle Rock with a commanding view of Scotland's capital, Edinburgh Castle is a historic fortress that has witnessed many significant events throughout Scottish history.

Along with its rich history, the castle is reputed to be one of the most haunted places in Scotland. Among the many spirits said to wander its halls, the most poignant and mysterious is perhaps that of the Drummer Boy.

The Haunting Melody

Legend has it that the ghost of a drummer boy haunts Edinburgh Castle, particularly during times of unrest. First sighted in the 1650s when Oliver Cromwell launched an attack against the Scots, the boy is said to play a haunting, rhythmic beat on his drum, echoing through the stone corridors. It's believed that his drumming serves as a warning of impending danger.

Who Was the Drummer Boy?

The identity of the Drummer Boy remains a mystery. Some stories suggest that he was a young boy sent into the castle's tunnels to drum a steady beat, helping soldiers to know the tunnel's direction as they dug. Tragically, it is said that he never emerged from the tunnels and that his drumming continued long after his disappearance, giving rise to the haunting legend.

The Tunnels Below

A significant part of the Drummer Boy legend involves the mysterious tunnels that stretch from Edinburgh Castle towards Holyrood Palace. These tunnels, discovered centuries later, were believed to be used for secret escapes and covert operations. The legend of the Drummer Boy is closely tied to these dark and eerie passageways.

Sightings and Sounds

Over the centuries, visitors, staff, and residents of Edinburgh Castle have reported hearing the distant sound of drumming, especially during times of war or political unrest. Despite extensive searches during these times, no source for the sound has ever been discovered, further deepening the mystery.

Edinburgh Castle Today

Today, Edinburgh Castle is one of Scotland's most visited tourist attractions. The staff are well-versed in its many ghost stories and are more than happy to share the tales with visitors. While the castle is a site of historical and architectural wonder, the legends and ghost stories, including that of the Drummer Boy, add an enticing layer of mystery that draws visitors from around the world.

The legend of the Drummer Boy of Edinburgh Castle is a haunting and enduring part of Scotland's folklore. Whether you consider it a mere tale or something more tangible, the story adds to the castle's atmospheric allure, making a visit to this historic fortress an even more unforgettable experience.

BRITISH GHOSTS

The Ghosts of Muncaster Castle

Standing proudly amidst the picturesque landscape of Cumbria, is the magnificent Muncaster Castle, a grand estate with a history stretching back over a thousand years.

Beyond its architectural splendor and stunning gardens, Muncaster Castle holds a darker reputation—it is renowned as one of the most haunted places in Britain.

The Headless Drummer

One of the most famous phantoms at Muncaster is the Headless Drummer. According to legend, during a feud between rival families in the 16th century, a young drummer boy was beheaded, and his body was thrown into a well. It is said that his ghost now roams the grounds, and the beating of his drum can be heard reverberating through the castle walls on stormy nights.

Tom Fool, the Castle's Sinister Jester

Perhaps the most infamous ghost of Muncaster Castle is Tom Fool, also known as Thomas Skelton. A court jester at Muncaster in the 16th century, Tom Fool was known for his dark sense of humor and cruel pranks. Legend has it that he committed murder during his time at the castle. Today, visitors report feeling an eerie sense of unease when entering the chamber known as 'Tom Fool's Window,' and some claim to have seen his mischievous figure skulking around the grounds.

The Weeping Lady

In the Tapestry Room, visitors and staff alike have reported the haunting cries of a woman, believed to be Mary Bragg, a young girl who worked at the castle in the early 19th century. Tragically, Mary was murdered in a love triangle gone awry. It is said that her ghost lingers in the room where she once slept, her sobs echoing through the night.

Paranormal Investigations

Muncaster Castle has long been a focal point for paranormal investigators. Numerous teams have explored the castle with an array of equipment, hoping to capture evidence of the supernatural. From mysterious cold spots to unexplained footsteps, the castle continues to be a magnet for those intrigued by the paranormal.

Muncaster Castle Today

Muncaster Castle is now a vibrant and popular tourist attraction. The Pennington family, who have been in residence for over 800 years, have lovingly maintained the property. Visitors are invited to explore the historic rooms, stunning gardens, and the Hawk and Owl Centre. The castle also embraces its haunted past with special ghost tours, particularly around Halloween.

So, if you find yourself in the Lake District, consider a visit to Muncaster Castle, and who knows? Perhaps you will encounter one of its famed spectral residents.

BRITISH GHOSTS

The Black Lady of Bradley Woods

Bradley Woods is a serene and picturesque location in the stunning countryside of Lincolnshire, famed for its natural beauty and tranquility.

However, beneath its peaceful veneer lies a chilling legend that has captivated the imagination of locals and visitors alike for centuries: the mysterious Black Lady of Bradley Woods.

The Legend Unveiled

According to local lore, the Black Lady is a ghostly figure who is said to haunt Bradley Woods, particularly on Christmas Eve. Dressed in a flowing black cloak, with her face obscured by a dark hood, she is often depicted as weeping inconsolably. Witnesses who have claimed to encounter her describe a profound sense of sorrow emanating from this spectral presence.

The Tragic Tale

The most popular version of the legend paints the Black Lady as the spirit of a young medieval woman. Her husband, a soldier, left for war, leaving her and their newborn child behind. After receiving news that her husband was killed in battle, the distraught woman is said to have wandered the woods in her grief until she herself passed away, leaving her spirit to roam in search of her lost love.

Sightings Through the Years

Over the years, numerous accounts have emerged from people who claim to have encountered the Black Lady of Bradley Woods. These sightings often involve a solitary figure, dressed in black, moving silently through the trees, her sorrow palpable. Such consistent and detailed reports have only served to fuel the legend, making it a significant part of local folklore.

A Symbol of Enduring Love?

Some interpretations of the legend view the Black Lady not as a figure to be feared, but as a poignant reminder of enduring love and loyalty. In this light, her eternal search through the woods is seen as a testament to the depth of her love for her husband and her longing for their reunion.

The Woods Today

Today, Bradley Woods is a popular spot for hikers, nature lovers, and families. The local authorities maintain the area beautifully, and it is rich with wildlife and natural scenery.

Despite its haunting legend—or perhaps because of it—Bradley Woods continues to be a beloved and frequently visited location.

BRITISH GHOSTS

The Hauntings of Dartmoor Prison

In the heart of the moody and mystical landscape of Dartmoor in Devon, stands a grim monument to justice and punishment: Dartmoor Prison.

Since its opening in 1809, this imposing structure has housed thousands of prisoners within its cold stone walls. As one of Britain's most notorious prisons, it is perhaps no surprise that Dartmoor is also reputed to be one of its most haunted locations.

A Brief History

Dartmoor Prison was originally built to house French prisoners of war during the Napoleonic era. It later became a place of incarceration for some of Britain's most hardened criminals. The prison's history is riddled with tales of brutal conditions, riots, and suffering, which some say have left a paranormal imprint.

The Ghost of Governor Rowe

One of the most famous ghosts of Dartmoor Prison is believed to be that of Governor Rowe, who died suddenly in 1812. It is said that his apparition, clad in period uniform, has been seen wandering the prison's corridors, a stern look on his face as he continues his rounds from the afterlife.

The Sobbing Specter

In the dark hours of the night, guards and inmates alike have reported hearing the heart-wrenching sobs of a man crying. Some believe this to be the spirit of a prisoner who was unjustly executed and whose grief lingers on in the stone walls of his former cell.

The Faceless Man

Another chilling tale is that of the faceless man—a shadowy figure that is often spotted in the older parts of the prison. Witnesses report an unsettling feeling of being watched, only to turn and see this dark, faceless entity, which vanishes as swiftly as it appears.

Paranormal Investigations

Dartmoor Prison has caught the attention of numerous paranormal investigators over the years. Armed with a variety of equipment, these teams have explored the eerie halls and cells of the prison, seeking evidence of the supernatural. From mysterious cold spots to unexplained noises and shadows, Dartmoor Prison remains a hotspot for potential paranormal activity.

Dartmoor Prison Today

Today, Dartmoor Prison continues to be a functioning correctional facility, albeit with much improved conditions compared to its grim past. The haunting stories, however, have become an indelible part of its identity, capturing the imagination of those who visit the surrounding area.

BRITISH GHOSTS

The Ghost Ship of Goodwin Sands

Off the coast of Kent, where the waters of the English Channel churn and swirl, lies a notorious maritime hazard known as the Goodwin Sands.

This extensive sandbank has been the site of countless shipwrecks over the centuries, giving it a grim reputation. Among the many stories that haunt these waters, the tale of the Ghost Ship of Goodwin Sands stands out as one of the most chilling and enduring.

The Treacherous Goodwin Sands

The Goodwin Sands are a shifting series of sandbanks located around six miles off the coast of Kent. Due to their position near the busy shipping routes of the English Channel, they have been the site of over 2,000 shipwrecks. This has earned them the nickname 'The Ship Swallower'.

The Legend of the Ghost Ship

The story revolves around a ghostly ship, said to appear in the midst of stormy weather near the Goodwin Sands. Witnesses have described it as a grand, 17th-century galleon, surrounded by a ghostly light, sailing smoothly despite the tumultuous sea. Then, as quickly as it appears, it vanishes into the mist, leaving no trace of its passage.

The Doomed Vessel

The most popular theory behind the identity of the ghost ship is that it is the 'Lady Lovibond,' a schooner that is said to have been wrecked on Goodwin Sands in 1748.

According to the tale, the ship's captain, Simon Peel, had just been married, and was celebrating with a cruise. In a tragic twist, the first mate, who was in love with the captain's wife, allegedly steered the ship into the sands in a fit of jealousy, sinking the ship and dooming all on board.

Sightings Through Time

Reports of the Ghost Ship of Goodwin Sands have surfaced regularly for centuries. In many cases, witnesses were unaware of the legend until after they reported their sighting. These consistencies lend an eerie credibility to the accounts. Some reports even come from seasoned mariners, further deepening the mystery.

A Warning or a Reminder?

For some, the appearance of the ghost ship is seen as a bad omen, a sign of impending doom for sailors. For others, it serves as a poignant reminder of the perilous nature of the sea and the human lives it has claimed throughout history.

Modern Investigations

The legend of the Ghost Ship of Goodwin Sands continues to intrigue paranormal investigators and maritime historians alike. Despite the advancement of technology, including radar and satellite imagery, sightings of the phantom vessel continue to be reported, defying logical explanation.

The Ghost Ship of Goodwin Sands is a captivating tale that adds a layer of mystery and intrigue to this already dramatic seascape.

As you stand on the Kentish shore, gazing out into the vast expanse of the English Channel, consider the mariners of old who navigated these treacherous waters—and perhaps keep an eye out for a spectral ship sailing amidst the storm.

BRITISH GHOSTS

FOLLOW US

www.facebook.com/darkhousepublishing